C000144406

Contents

FOREWORD

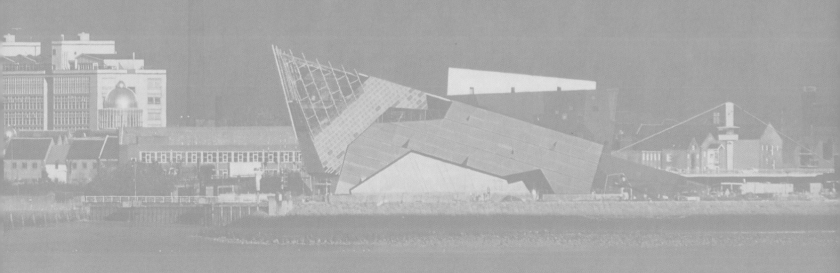

by The Rt Hon John Prescott, Deputy Prime Minister and MP for Hull East since 1983

Foreword

The opening of The Deep, Hull's £45.5m Millennium Commission lottery project, heralds the beginning of a new era for the pioneering city of Hull and its people. A landmark building, The Deep represents the renaissance, regeneration and aspirational spirit that flows through the veins of the city and its citizens.

The building is not only a wonderful piece of architecture, designed by world-class architect Sir Terry Farrell, but also a tremendous economic boost to the area. The Deep has many functions: as a tourist attraction, a lifelong learning centre, a business centre of excellence and an important research centre run in conjunction with the University of Hull.

The Deep is fundamental to realising the dream of urban regeneration for the people of Hull. Located at the meeting point of the rivers Hull and Humber, it is a symbol of Hull's age-old relationship with the sea and its increasingly close links with Europe. Signifying the changing face of the city, it is the first physical realisation of the massive urban regeneration taking place in Hull, building on its role as one of Europe's most important maritime trading ports.

With funding supplied from a variety of sources – the Lottery through the Millennium Commission, the Regional Development Agency, local government, European Regional Development and SRB funding – Hull has shown that it has the ability to build partnerships and deliver a complex project with national and international impact. And The Deep is only the beginning. There are many significant projects taking place in the city. Their common theme is a partnership between the public and private sectors.

As with The Deep, strategic sites of economic significance are being earmarked for change, to stimulate growth, investment and confidence to fulfil the aspirations of this great city. Following on from the £45.5m investment into The Deep, Kingston upon Hull City Council and the Regional Development Agency, Yorkshire Forward, are investing a further £150m in the Ferensway Development with their partners London & Amsterdam.

The Ferensway Development is a mixed-use scheme comprising a magnificent transport interchange designed by the award-winning Wilkinson Eyre Architects, along with over 200 residential homes and a retail and leisure complex designed by Foster & Partners. This site will also house the celebrated Hull Truck Theatre, home of playwright John Godber.

There is a real momentum to improve the city of Hull through culture, with the ever-expanding and improving museums quarter, tourism through major attractions such as The Deep, lifelong learning with the Children's University and new technology and the media, for example by the BBC using Hull's unique broadband capacity provided by Kingston Interactive Television, a subsidiary of Kingston Communications plc, with an investment of £25m for a state-of-the-art studio and training centre. The BBC has shown a real vote of confidence in the city by selecting Hull as its new regional headquarters.

Sport is also playing an important part in regeneration and Hull City Council has invested £43.5m in a new Community Super Stadium. A brand-new, world-class 25,000 capacity home for Hull City Football Club and Hull FC Rugby League Club, a concert venue, an indoor sports hall, BMX skate park and an extensive range of community sports, the stadium will be a fantastic resource for the people of Hull.

Finally, Hull is in the final stages of a proposed URC bid which, if successful, will be a vehicle for delivering long-term economic change through a programme of public and private investment in the city centre, the West Hull area and Riverside. It will create the right market conditions to make Hull a more competitive city, with the necessary infrastructure and employment skills to sustain it into the 21st century.

The city of Hull is a place I am proud to call home because of its pioneering nature, its aspiration and its pride. To my mind there is no better place to build The Deep.

John Prescott

5

THE GENESIS OF THE DEEP:
ORIGINS AND

We wanted to show people we were serious about The Deep. We wanted to show places like Hull could have a quality building. From the start I said I wanted something like the Sydney Opera House or the Eiffel Tower, something people could immediately identify as being in Hull and belonging to Hull.

Councillor David Gemmell

CONCEPT

HULL

The Genesis of The Deep

The City of Kingston upon Hull had suffered post-industrial trauma more than most cities in the UK. Work patterns were shifting: the huge industry devoted to ships and fishing was in retreat. The oldest of the city's central docks, dating from the late 18th century, was closed and filled in as early as 1935, and others fell empty and stayed that way until the start of the 1980s, when marine leisure and retail uses and housing began to colonise the area. Very badly blitzed during the Second World War, saddled with one of Patrick Abercrombie's less inspired post-war reconstruction plans, and with a huge amount of its housing concentrated in fringe council estates, the city retained a wounded feel. At the centre, a vacuum was left, especially when short-hop ferry activity across to Lincolnshire from Victoria Pier ceased with the opening in 1981 of the superbly graceful Humber Bridge, sited upstream of the city. The original heart of the city – its reason for existing – fell silent.

Some years before, the reclusive poet Philip Larkin had chosen Hull for his base: not least, as he remarked, since very few American students could ever find their way there to bother him, but also because he was simply fond of the place and its unaffected character. In recent times, Central Hull has revived, in particular the historic quarter located in the streets behind the Victoria Pier. Compounding the sense of isolation caused by the cessation of the cross-Humber ferry trade, for 20 years this area had

suffered from being cut off by an inner ring road – a late fragment of Abercrombie-building. Despite the continuing barrier of this road, buildings that were boarded-up wrecks a few years back are now turning into apartment buildings and restaurants. Plans for a pedestrian link bridge across this traffic corridor by architects Wilkinson Eyre will now help to heal the scar.

Further out from the centre, marine-related industries are still present in reasonable concentration, while on the macro-economic scale the city's importance is (as, it could be argued, was always the case) now more European than British. Commercial and tourist traffic from across the North Sea has continued to increase with the opening of new terminals to service some of the biggest new ferries in existence. So while Hull may be thought to be isolated from a British – specifically southern British – point of view, from a European perspective it is well situated on a key east-west trade route running from Russia to Ireland. It thus still has as much to do with the sea as the land.

Then Hull received an extraordinary windfall. Due to the foresight of the city fathers, Hull had retained its own telecommunications network, a throwback to the days before nationalisation. Kept at the forefront of technology, this city-owned company proved to be a lucrative investment, yielding rich rewards in the late 1990s when it was part-privatised

as Kingston Communications. The city finally had the wherewithal to consider long-term planning strategy rather than the piecemeal improvements that had taken place until then. Terry Farrell and Partners' River Hull Corridor masterplan, also known as Hull 2020, came after the commission for The Deep and is a result of this climate of self-awareness in the city. Many of the points it makes relate to history.

The city had been founded at the confluence of the small but navigable River Hull and the expanse of the Humber estuary. An imaginary bird's-eye view of 1640 by Wenceslaus Hollar shows what is essentially the core of the city today, cradled in the right-angle between the two rivers and surrounded by a city wall that extended eastwards to enclose land beyond the River Hull and fortify the city against invasion. There were powerful historic reasons, then, for the masterplan to consider broadly the same area originally depicted by Hollar. The chosen site for The Deep, Sammy's Point, sits right on the confluence of the two rivers but on the reclaimed eastern side, a few yards south of where Hollar had shown a sizeable defensive bastion on the eastern city wall, and where later a large triangular citadel had been built to defend the city against possible Dutch invasion.

Later still, the area became industrial. Sammy's Point is named after Martin Samuelson, a 19th century shipbuilder and local politician whose yard

covered the 12 acre point, part reclaimed land, where ships swing into the mouth of the Hull from the Humber. Historian John Markham – to whom I am indebted – recounts that Samuelson was a typically ebullient Victorian entrepreneur: born in Hamburg in 1825, early career as a railway engineer, then moving to Hull in 1849 to take over an iron foundry which, in those expansionist times and given the maritime might of the city, led logically and swiftly to iron shipbuilding. At that time, only Liverpool was growing faster than Hull. In 1854, aged only 29, Samuelson launched his first ship, the Irwell. By 1859 he had built 40. A small energetic figure in colourful clothes more reminiscent of Regency times, he was always to be seen scurrying around the city, checking up on his various engineering businesses. Accounts of the time refer to the River Hull bristling with iron ships at various stages of construction. The great triangular citadel – for centuries a landmark here – was first colonised by the space-hungry new industries of Sammy and others, then in 1864 demolished.

"Sammy" Samuelson became an important civic figure, served as mayor, and applied himself to one of the major preoccupations of any 19th century city: improving sanitation. But again typically of the period, he over-reached himself, found himself financially exposed by the bankruptcy of a shipowner client, Zachariah Pearson, was himself declared bankrupt

Hull retains its fishing tradition.

In the 1800s, Hull was a vibrant trading port.

Ferry to Goxhill looking to Sammy's Point.

Historical map of the city.

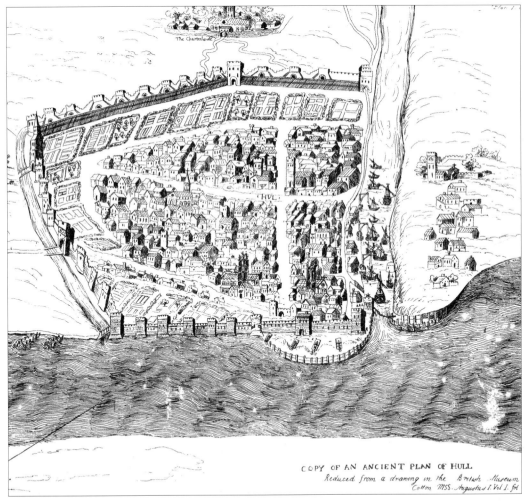

COPY OF AN ANCIENT PLAN OF HULL
Reduced from a drawing in the British Museum
Cotton MSS. Augustus I. Vol I. fol

Historical view of the walled city.

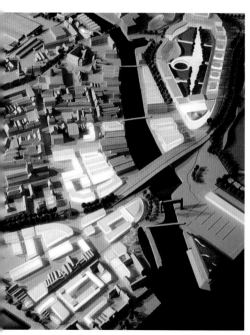

TFP masterplan prepared for Hull CityVision.

and was forced to sell up. But when he died in 1903 at the age of 78, he was still working as an engineer, employed by the Humber Conservancy and apparently still conversant with new technology: half an hour before his death he was to be seen talking on the telephone to one of his clerks.

In 1833, three men established a shipyard on what was later to become part of Samuelson's site. The company they started subsequently became the well-known shipbuilding firm of Cook Welton & Gemmell. The latter, William Gemmell, was the son of a family who had come to Hull from Glasgow. As a young man Gemmell served his apprenticeship as a shipwright and later worked as a draughtsman and naval architect at Earle's Shipyard. He was also the great-great-great uncle of David Gemmell, who initiated The Deep project in 1995.

The area east of the River Hull remained largely industrial: the rebuilding of the centre in Edwardian times and the inter-war years, with some glorious civic buildings, followed Hull's tardy designation as a city in 1898 – but this activity stopped at the natural boundary of the little river, which remained a natural harbour off the sometimes stormy estuary, and a conduit for maritime industries reaching upstream as far as Beverley, where small ships were built and launched. Thus, when the traditional industries of the city closed down, Sammy's Point was left as a very prominent disused site, the southern termination of

a corridor of decline around the River Hull. While the remaining old central docks to the west had already been revived reasonably successfully with a marina, housing, and a new shopping centre, this eastern fringe was more problematic.

The City, in starting to think about its long-term future, began by inviting in the corporate identity consultants Wolff Olins. This early research confirmed the need (expressed as early as 1993) for a visitor attraction that would tag the city in people's minds, would be the equivalent of the Liver Building, or Newcastle's bridges, or Sydney's opera house (the Bilbao Guggenheim, now acknowledged as one of the best examples of "cultural regeneration" of a neglected city, was not at that stage built). But the two people who were to be instrumental in getting The Deep built – Councillor David Gemmell, chair of the city's tourism committee, and the city's director of leisure Colin Brown – began to think around the subject. Hull was known for its cultural events and festivals, but had reached a ceiling on those. What it lacked was indeed a single, must-see cultural magnet. What should it be? And how should it be paid for?

The first idea was a museum: more specifically, one that could be an outstation of one of the big London museums. A new art gallery was rejected – the Tate already had its Liverpool satellite, and moreover Hull already possessed the excellent Ferens art gallery with its fine contemporary track record. Hartlepool, further north, was in discussion with the Imperial War Museum: another possibility. But the IWM eventually settled on Manchester. The Royal Armouries were going to Leeds, in a controversial pre-Lottery public-private partnership arrangement. Given Hull's seafaring history, another good fit might have been the National Maritime Museum, but that, like the Tate, already had its outstation long established in Liverpool. The Victoria and Albert Museum had also established looser ties with other cities. But there was a gap in the regional-museum market: there was no equivalent satellite of the Natural History Museum. Gemmell and Brown travelled down to London to discuss the idea with the NHM, which gave a positive response – but had no money to bring to the table and, somewhat surprisingly, had no spare exhibits to farm out.

On the train back, the two men agreed that they felt that the oceanographic side of natural history was not particularly well served in the London museum. Thus the seed of what eventually became The Deep was born: could not Hull go it alone, with a natural history museum of the sea? This was blue-sky stuff. It was 1995, the city council was effectively broke, the private sector was not interested in speculative cultural buildings in Hull. And then, like some Brechtian god descending, the National Lottery was born.

It was quickly established that the Millennium Commission was the only possible lottery distributor for such a project, since it would not qualify for Arts Council or Heritage lottery funding. The catch was that – unlike those others – the Millennium Commission granted a maximum 50 per cent of the cost of its approved projects, come what may. Which still left an awful lot of matching money to find – without which, the Commission would not cough up anything at all. First guess was a building costing £25m. Soon this seemed unrealistic. To have the

 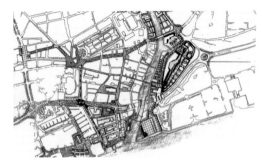

TFP's masterplan developed an urban design approach for the whole of Hull.

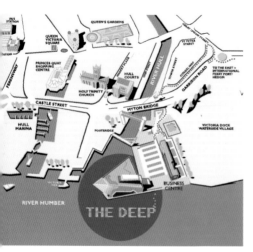

The Deep is the only building of significance to acknowledge the waterfront.

necessary magnet effect, the building and its content had to be above a certain scale. The notional price rose to £37m and was to rise more. Gemmell also insisted that whatever was built should start its operational life totally debt-free, without punishing bank loans to pay off.

Parallel with the search for funding was the search for the best site. A possible location on the western edge of the city was rejected on the grounds that it would bring visitors only as far as the outskirts, not into the centre where they were needed. The central but run-down street of Ferensway was briefly considered (this was later to become the focus of an ambitious commercial redevelopment plan designed by Lord Foster). Another site closer in, but still west of the Victoria Pier, was also a candidate. Then the council leader, Pat Doyle, suggested the derelict Sammy's Point. The council owned the land, but it had been earmarked for fair-rent and student housing. This, it was beginning to be felt, was a waste of a site with enormous potential. Moreover, if the council donated the land, that would count towards the vital matching funding, as would money from the European regional development fund. Then the University of Hull chipped in with its idea for a research and educational maritime centre – and brought with it access to research funds. The University entered into partnership with the council. The idea was taking off.

With the plan loosely described as "the evolving sea", soon the idea of a 21st-century aquarium entered the mix. A concept plan was drawn up. Gemmell and Brown studied the rapidly-emerging Millennium Dome in London, admired some of the exhibition designers, but realised that the whole thing was structured the wrong way round – first the building, then the exhibition designers, finally the ideas. The Deep was to work the other way round: the content was to come first. "If we had done the first thing we thought of," Gemmell says today, "It would not have turned out one-tenth as good."

By the time the scheme was submitted for Millennium Commission approval in 1997, Brown's working title of "The Deep" was beginning to stick. This was to be one of the last of the Commission's "landmark" projects, intended to join such company as the Eden Project in Cornwall, Tate Modern in London, the Centre for Life in Newcastle (another Farrell project) Magna and the Earth Centre in South Yorkshire, the Lowry theatre/art gallery complex in Salford, the Glasgow Science Centre, Leicester Space Centre and so forth. Most of these had been approved long previously but in this round, The Deep felt itself to be in competition with Magna – a redundant steelworks in Rotherham to be converted into a "science adventure centre". The Millennium Commission liked a good geographical spread of its projects – was Magna too close for comfort?

Early concept study of buildings on the promontory.

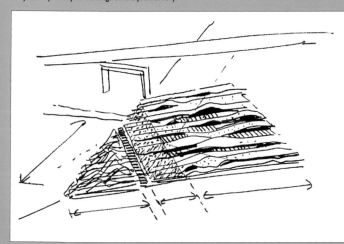

Early concept for landscape design.

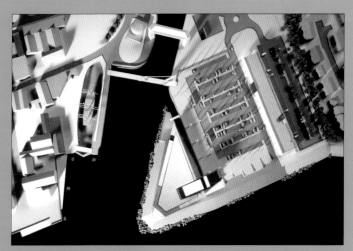

View of the masterplan model.

The local press was a vociferous supporter of the project – something that was not always the case with other such bids – which helped. The Commission, in the shape of commissioner Sir John Hall, was beady-eyed and inclined to ask searching and awkward questions. Gemmell recalls one "really long, hard and hectic meeting". But this also helped, since Sir John, once satisfied, became an ally. But it was still an anxious time as the bids were whittled down from an original 1,000 or so to 100, then ten. Finally the news came through. Both Magna and The Deep had succeeded. The Deep had £18.4m of Millennium cash towards what was then a £37m project. And there was still no building designed. That was the next step.

In the subsequent 1998 architectural competition, which came down to a shortlist of six ranging from young hopefuls to famous names, Terry Farrell's design "stood out head and shoulders" above the rest, according to Gemmell. It best fulfilled the criterion of being an aspirational, landmark building suited to the programme of the exhibition it would contain. It was also – this was seen as important – a building that would tell a story. It was narrative architecture that would form part of the exhibition, inside and out. And it responded to the working title: it had to be deep, both in the sense of emphasising physical depth and in going well beyond the superficial in its handling of the subject. As Colin

Brown is apt to say, it was not to be just another fish museum. An aquarium was to be part of it, but by no means all of it.

As usual with Farrell, the surroundings were extensively considered. He pushed the building right to the edge of the Humber for maximum effect. He regarded a pedestrian bridge from The Deep across the River Hull to the historic centre as vital. In his subsequent River Hull masterplan, covering 380 hectares of the city centre and its eastern side, Farrell was to extend this to a series of connections linking east with west, allowing car parking to move out of its present mish-mash of cleared sites in the centre (some of them, amazingly, still Second World War bomb sites) over the Hull, so freeing up the central sites for rebuilding the urban fabric. A new cultural quarter, business centre and park is envisaged east of the Hull (and north of The Deep). Equally crucial to the plan – though perhaps rather harder to achieve – is the removal of the ghastly barrier of the 1982 southern ring road, replacing it with a pedestrian-friendly boulevard and light rail system. There is much else to the plan, but those are the two key moves intended to relieve the present constricting corset around the heart of the city. The plan is intended to be implemented in phases up to the year 2020. In the meantime, The Deep had to act as a magnet with no other aid than its own pedestrian bridge – and that was delayed some

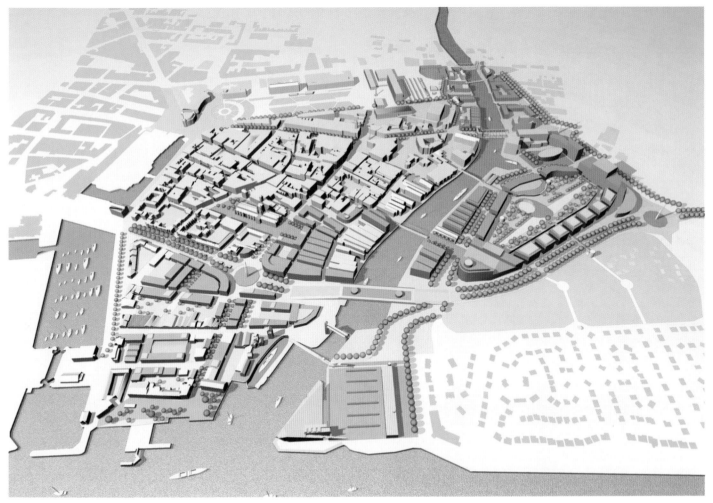

The Deep is part of TFP's River Hull Corridor Masterplan.

six months after the opening, owing to an unforeseen dispute over navigation clearance in the River Hull. The enterprise could at least console itself with the thought that the equivalent, if rather larger, pedestrian bridge across the Thames to Tate Modern in London was delayed by two years as its embarrassing wobble was rectified.

What made the financial sums add up in the end – especially when the project increased in ambition and budget to its final £45.5m – was the way that the city underwrote the project's cash flow. This was made easier once it had received its huge windfall from Kingston Communications, but it was always a courageous move. Essentially, the city provided a £4.4m loan facility on top of its donation of the land and some other incidentals, in all amounting to £5.4m. The Millennium Commission's input eventually totalled £21.48 million, the European Regional Development Fund £7.74m, the government's Single Regeneration budget £3.8m, and the "Yorkshire Forward" consortium £3.37m. Smaller sums came from the University of Hull and the Garfield Weston Foundation. The last £3m of funding came from an innovative finance leasing transaction – The Deep is grateful to the National Australia Bank, Capstar Partners Limited and Druces & Attlee Solicitors for their invaluable expertise in bringing this to fruition.

The running costs of the venture are helped by the success of Farrell's business centre – always a part of the proposal, though a further money-generating idea for the site, namely a youth hostel, was vetoed by the Commission. The upshot of it all is that The Deep opened clear of debt as Gemmell and Brown always wanted, and with a deliberately low break-even figure for visitor numbers, even with a modest entry charge of £6, or £4 for children. Research by consultants Coopers and Lybrand had yielded projected figures ranging from a "pessimistic" 250,000 a year to an "optimistic" 450,000. There is something very Yorkshire about the way Gemmell and Brown decided to be even more cautious, holding the break-even figure to around 200,000. Anything more than that will be seen as a bonus and will yield useful operational profit. Both men had learned from the catastrophic PR of the Millennium Dome, which despite its huge numbers of visitors came to be branded a failure because its break-even point – and consequent massaged visitor projections – were both unrealistically high.

The public response to The Deep has a bearing on more than just its own operational budget, however. If it does well, it will undoubtedly hasten the regeneration of the entire area. Many hopes rest upon its muscular shoulders.

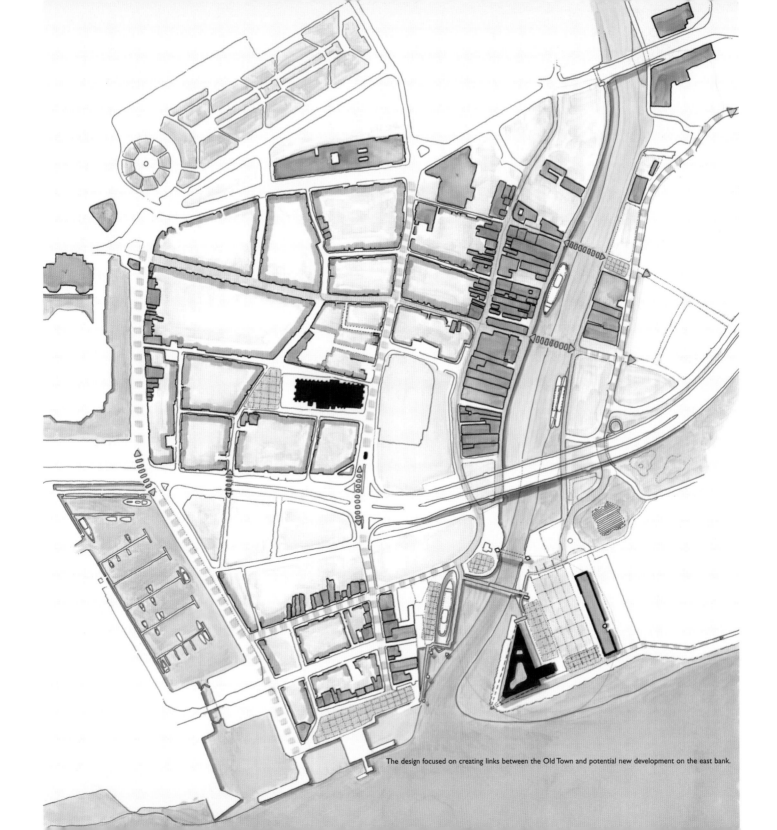

The design focused on creating links between the Old Town and potential new development on the east bank.

THE DEEP:
HOW THE
DESIGN

EVOLVED

The Deep is integral to the infrastructure of the River Hull corridor, as well as the economic, social and cultural renewal of the city. The flat openness of the site and its dramatic seascape views led us towards the image of a geological monolith whose fractures and fault lines create a complex pattern over its surface. The dramatic ascent of the building as it rises out of the ground is a symbol of regeneration and optimism that recalls the pioneering spirit of Hull.

Sir Terry Farrell, Terry Farrell & Partners

How the design evolved

A coral atoll.

The main tank is designed to hold large fish.

Design concept image.

The design of The Deep as a piece of architecture ran through several iterations – for instance, there was an early concept scheme by other designers that took the form of a symmetrical curving hull-like form – but once Terry Farrell & Partners had won the competition in late 1998 for what was by then a Millennium Commission funded scheme, it always stayed true to its two essential design principles. Externally, the building was conceived as a geological shard, rising to a sharp point right at the seaward end of the site. Internally, it was composed as a series of voids around the immovable central object of the largest, deepest, tank. But beyond those two fixed points, pinning down the design and meeting the budget required some substantial shifts in thinking along the way.

Looking at the building now, it all seems very assured and – for such a striking shape – logical, but the existence of the built work in this form was anything but inevitable. You might equally imagine, for instance, that a marine-based visitor attraction could take its imagery from the waves or from the creatures in them, that there would be a clear aqueous or organic metaphor rather than a geological one. And you might think, also, that the all-important central tank in such a super-aquarium might be regarded as a hollow element for the purposes of design. Not least because it is hollow, and because you can obviously see right into it from various viewpoints.

There are many reasons to explain the final appearance of the building – the broadly triangular shape of Sammy's Point, for instance, which in an earlier time had helped to generate the triangular defensive citadel, not demolished until the 1860s, very close by. There was also a prominent slipway on the site, the memory of which is kept in the moat of water running along the approach at the eastern side of the building and which also gives it a fortified feel. Then, too, there was the desire to create a vantage point from which to view the city, the Humber Bridge, the sea and the sky. Nothing so clichéd as an observation tower was ever mooted, and it is odd to think that the viewing level was a relatively late arrival in the design process anyway, but the upwardly tilting form that evolved seemed naturally to develop into a panoramic nose-cone.

But how did that form come about? Farrell talks of the idea of glaciers and their terminal moraines, of the fact that the great ice-sheet of the last ice age had its edge around here. He then connects this with the idea of fossil remains. There was a fish, for instance, beloved of paleontologists and Darwinian evolutionists alike, that found itself trapped in progressively shallower waters as the ice sheet retreated. Over a surprisingly short time on the evolutionary scale, it evolved from a vertically organised fish into a flatfish, eventually becoming very flat indeed, a kind of mudflapper. All of its stages are

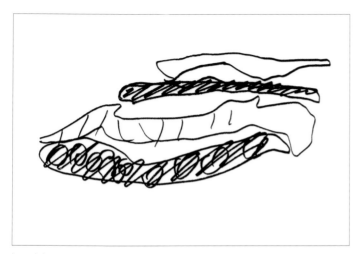

Layered elements.

People inhabit the voids.

The design bears a resemblance to *The Ice Sea* by German Romantic painter Caspar David Friedrich.

The barrenness of the site led TFP towards a free and imaginative form.

recorded in the sedimentary and metamorphic rocks of the area. For Farrell, this fish was a useful conceptual lever. The history of the seas, he realised, is enshrined in geological history. If a tectonic movement raises a fragment of the earth's crust, the oceans of antiquity are revealed.

So the design drew together these various complementary strands. A peninsula with a memory of a fortified, angular building, commanding the seaways: the idea of the southern termination of an ice sheet, like a glacier's edge as it meets the sea; the related but different idea of a geological monolith, a cliff-like slice of sedimentary rock rearing up from the ground, its layers and fissures clearly apparent; and the treatment of the central feature of the building – the largest tank – as a solid object, a huge boulder of water, around which people would move like potholers, in crevasses and caverns. Some of the very earliest design sketches are not of the exterior form of the building at all, but are a schematic of spaces being carved out of a solid object.

Some aspects of all this had been explored previously by the Farrell office in its design for a new National Aquarium in London's Royal Docks (unbuilt but, at the time of writing, in the process of being revived). In that case, the design was a more conventional modified box. Here, the design solution evolved into something more radical. This suited the demands of the client. It had long been established,

from the earliest "branding" studies carried out for the city by consultants Wolff Olins, that Hull needed more than just regeneration of buildings and activities, more than a mere visitor attraction. After all, a bowling alley in a tin shed would fulfill those criteria. No, what Hull wanted was that old standby, a landmark piece of architecture, something that would put the city back on the map for the 21st century. A place that would do for Hull what the opera house did for Sydney, or the Guggenheim did for Bilbao.

This, of course, was also a key requirement of the Millennium Commission which provided £21.48m of the £45.5m cost of the project, by far the largest single chunk of finance. Thus everybody was thinking along the same lines but as Farrell points out, such concepts can easily go awry unless there is a firmly committed client prepared to stand a modicum of risk. To which it might be added that, unless there is a clear and strong concept when it comes to the content of such attractions, architects are working in a void. In plenty of Lottery-funded projects, there is surprisingly little contact between architect and client body, and surprisingly little idea of what the building is actually for. The best built examples are always those where there is both an identifiable and involved client. In this case, Farrell recalls, he knew that things augured well when the client body – represented throughout by Councillor David Gemmell and the city council's then director

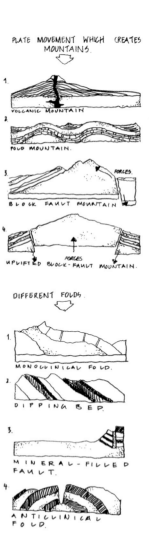

PLATE MOVEMENT WHICH CREATES MOUNTAINS.

1. VOLCANIC MOUNTAIN
2. FOLD MOUNTAIN.
3. BLOCK FAULT MOUNTAIN
4. UPLIFTED BLOCK-FAULT MOUNTAIN.

DIFFERENT FOLDS.

1. MONOCLINICAL FOLD.
2. DIPPING BED.
3. MINERAL-FILLED FAULT.
4. ANTICLINICAL FOLD.

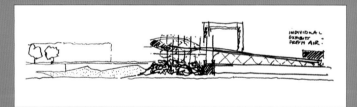

Concept sketch showing building relationships.

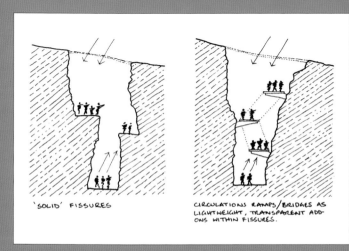

'SOLID' FISSURES

CIRCULATIONS RAMPS/BRIDGES AS LIGHTWEIGHT, TRANSPARENT ADD ONS WITHIN FISSURES.

Design development of geological fissure metaphor, used to inform spaces and movement within the building.

INDIVIDUAL EXHIBITS FRESH AIR.

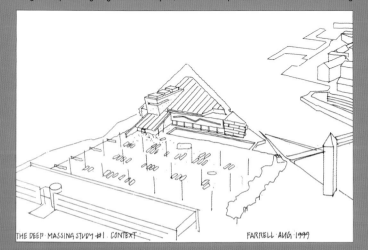

THE DEEP MASSING STUDY #1 CONTEXT   FARRELL AUG. 1999

Early study of the aquarium as vessel.

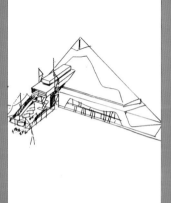

Design studies of entrance tower.

25

Section through concept model.

of leisure Colin Brown – crystallised into a logical structure. Gemmell, later made chairman, gave Farrell his home phone number and told him to call any time, day or night, to discuss the scheme. Gemmell and Brown, who was in charge of the project, were to prove a valuable sounding-board as the design developed.

Farrell also benefited by knowing, at the stage of his appointment, exactly what the building was for and what it had to do. There was still work to be done on the exhibition design, but the idea of the uber-aquarium (later called a "submarium" by Brown) was strong and immediate. Also by that time the University of Hull was on board with its own programme for a marine research centre, which forms part of the main building just off the public areas. Farrell remarks that several of the best and most successful Millennium Projects are those that revive and develop Victorian ideas: such as the great botanical "glasshouses" of Sir Nicholas Grimshaw's Eden Project in Cornwall. The public aquarium with research function is also essentially a Victorian idea, but in this case moved forward into something much more: not just a place to see fish in tanks, but a place to explore the whole concept of the oceans and what they mean to us.

The first Farrell design – generally known as the "glacier" version, influenced by a particular painting of Caspar David Friedrich (see page 23) – was

publicly revealed in February 1999. This had been through some intensive modelling by Simon Baker and was to receive much more from Farrell and his partner Aidan Potter as the battle began to make the scheme fit the money available. The pronounced overhang at the tip of the building, for instance, was a potentially very costly indulgence: how to make it work within the budget? A way was found, with the scheme becoming more snub-nosed and the cladding details less sinuous, more tectonic.

As site reclamation work began in March 1999, and with Bovis Lend Lease, the chosen management contractor, coming in October to begin the piling work for the new building, things were by then moving fast. Slightly too fast for comfort, in fact, because contracts had to be let on the basis of a still-evolving design. Why the hurry? Because Hull had been told – as had all recipients of Millennium Commission largesse – that the scheme had to be up and running by 2001 at the latest – the correct Millennium year, if you are being pedantic, since 2000 was actually the final year of the old Millennium rather than the first of the new.

As one of the last Millennium Commission schemes to be approved in the last tranche of grants for such large-scale projects, this meant moving with some haste to meet the deadline. Later, of course, it transpired that the deadline was flexible to the extent that the scheme qualified even if only part

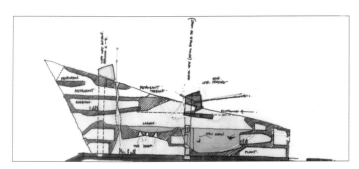

Early concept drawings.

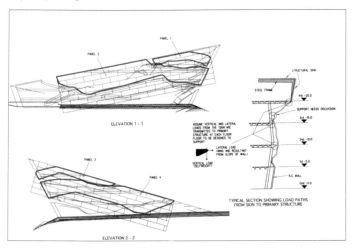

Early concept drawings of steel plate cladding.

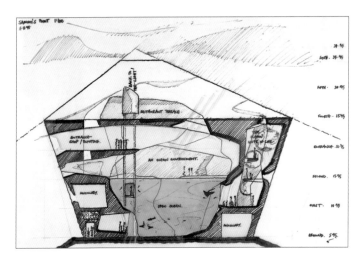

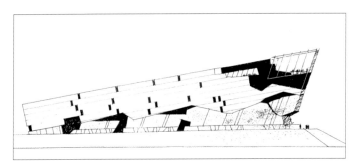

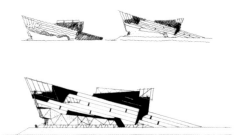

Early colour studies.

of it was in operation in the relevant year. Since the separate revenue-generating business centre, a simple two-storey strip of rentable office space set east of the main building, was opened by Prime Minister Tony Blair during 2001, this criterion applied, so allowing The Deep to be completed in time for Easter 2002. However, in the early stages this convenient outcome could not be forecast, and consequently there was some conflict between the demands of a rapid construction programme, and the need to hone the design to its desirable conclusion.

Accordingly there came a moment, towards the end of 1999, when client and design team decided to make some fairly radical changes in order to deliver the building as they wished it to be – and this required certain of the already-nominated contractors to abandon what they thought they were going to build and adjust their thinking.

Two aspects were involved, and again, one was external and one internal. Externally, both architect and client wished to develop the arrangement of the complex cladding details. The aim was always to make it look as if it was an object rising out of the ground: the danger was that unless the detailing of the cladding was done just so, it might seem the reverse – a building slipping into the ground, a vessel sinking beneath the waves. This was not an image that Hull, after all the consideration it had given to

the regenerative and symbolic importance of its new landmark building, wanted to risk happening.

At the same time the decision was made to incorporate the intensive services needed by a large-scale aquarium within the building rather than remotely (the early idea had been to site this equipment below the ground level "moat" on the eastern side). The change meant shorter runs of pipe and ductwork, much easier maintenance access, and lower costs. But because of the extra weight the building would have to carry at high level, this impacted considerably on the steelwork structure of the building, as did the changed cladding details.

Both Farrell and his clients talk of the "Boxing Day drawings" that he produced at this stage, in a burst of concentration away from the office. This finally fixed the external appearance of the building, especially the pattern of its complex, layered cladding. The size of the main cladding sheets – originally envisaged as stainless steel – was reduced to the largest available panels of marine-grade aluminium, as used in shipbuilding. These were given a rhomboidal form, implying a movement upwards and outwards. The milling marks on the panels also helped in the patterning process. The gradation of colour in the back-enamelled glass panels towards the peak of the building was also refined considerably at this point.

The "Boxing Day drawings" did the trick.

28

Early concept sequence showing the erosion of the monolith.

1 Upheaval of land creates monolith

2 Ground fault fractures
   Principal fault lines apparent

3 Major fissures created
   Erosion starts
   Wind/rain
   First material from monolith falls at base

4 Fissures enlarge
   Greater definition of fissures
   Flood water erosion by stream
   Revetment material builds up

5 Minor fissures created
   Further erosion around and into base of building
   Revetment as a defined form
   Roof erosion defined

6 Man's intervention
   Access/habitability
   Regularisation of lines of erosion

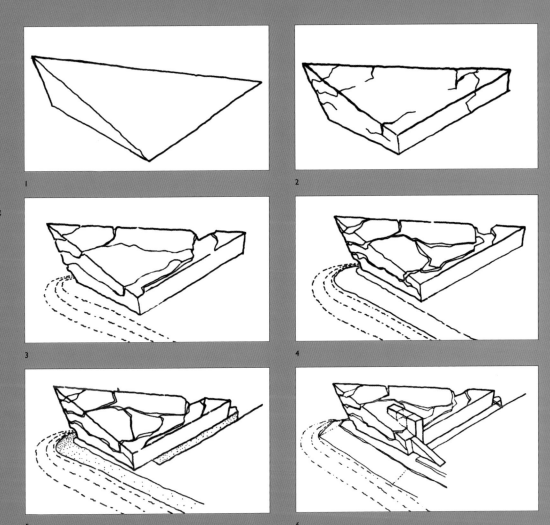

1

2

3

4

5

6

The design was all but complete, the necessary adjustments were made, work could continue with confidence. You see the outcome most clearly in the western façade of the building, facing Victoria Pier. This elevation plays a considerable architectural game. It completely disguises the fact that The Deep is essentially a "black box" – the ideal exhibition environment because of the lack of distraction from the displays – with windows only at the very top of the prow, and in the non-display areas on the eastern side. Since the entrance is also on the eastern side, this very prominent western façade is in reality the back of the building, despite the fact that a new pedestrian swing bridge (not designed by Farrell) connects The Deep across the River Hull to the city centre at this point. The effect of the layered and textured façade, with its angles and fissures and constantly-changing colours and reflections, is to overcome the necessary blindness of such exhibition boxes.

This is the key to the architectural rationale of The Deep. Farrell, being no dogmatic modernist, has never been one to deny the place of decoration in architecture, but here it serves a very particular purpose: the animation and proportioning of the building's main elevation as seen from the city, so making it a place of mystery and possibility. Clear glass and exposed steel structure, pearlescent back-enamelled coloured glass, silver-grey marine-grade aluminium and striated, painted in-situ concrete form the palette of materials.

A similar treatment is given to the shorter return elevation, running along the Humber's edge, on the far side of the triangulated prow. The slightly outward-leaning walls and equally slight offset to the nose-cone yield some interesting geometrical effects as you round the prow. But the entrance elevation of the building, facing the long horizontal block of the business centre, is a very different beast. There are offices and education rooms and back-of-house support facilities and tanks here, yielding a random pattern of fenestration that the Farrell office calls "the hokey-cokey windows". The entrance is pulled forward as a separate wing. A cylindrical "skimmer tower", housing water cleaning equipment, breaks through the roofline. Given that there are different activities taking place on this side of the building, and given the different context it faces (close to its own business centre and a recent docklands housing development rather than longer views across to more civic buildings and spaces), the architecture is handled accordingly. This is most notable in its softer surface treatment, which makes much use of self-coloured render and is generally more approachable, less the jagged landmark.

Inside, the exhibition design by John Csáky Associates spins off from the building, almost literally. The route the visitor takes was determined by Farrell and his clients: unusually, you both start and finish your visit nearly at the top. From the lobby, you whizz

Study models assessing cladding and internal features.

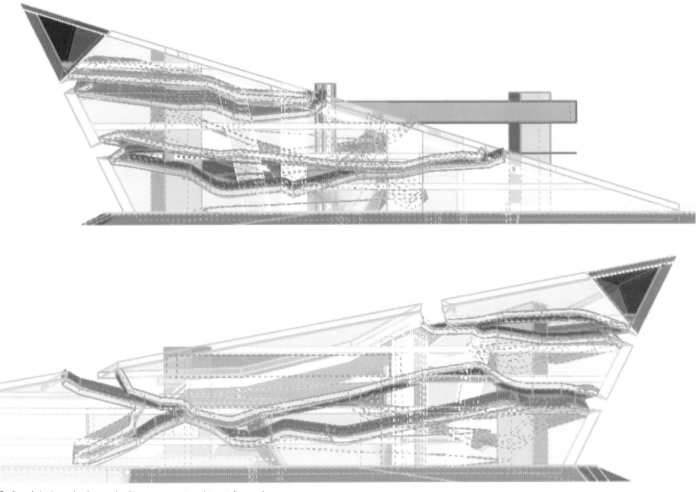

Studies relating internal and external architectures to create an integrated expression.

up to the penultimate floor in a conventional dark lift, stepping out into daylight and great views out. Then you spiral down through the exhibition, back and forth, side to side, down to the very bottom – passing through time the deeper you go. Finally you shoot back up in a scenic lift, riding through the big central tank that you have glimpsed at various points on your descent. At the top there is the café and, a level above that, a smaller floor in the tip of the building, leading out onto the viewing gallery in the point. When you've taken in the panorama of waterscape and cityscape, it's back to the ground floor and out. Thus the building's architecture, always conceived with the programme of its functions in mind, presented the readymade bare bones of the exhibition layout. Content and container are interdependent.

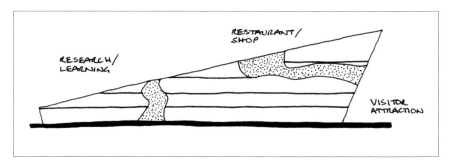

3 elements.

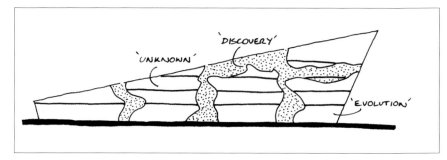

3 elements + visitor attraction theme.

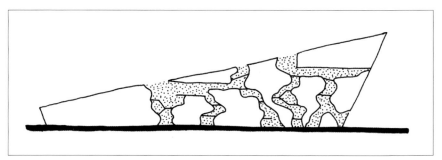

All visitor attraction circulation.

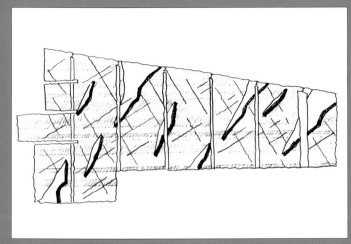

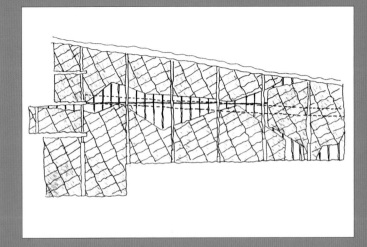

Internal wall elevation design studies.

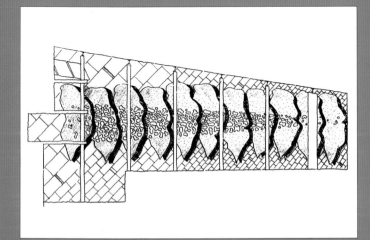

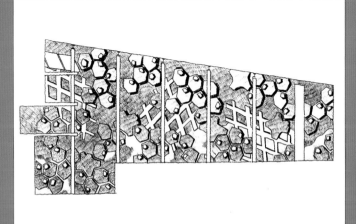

Computer model perspective of the glazed observation point.

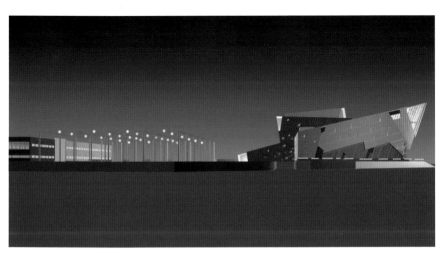

Night-time colour studies. Perspective from the River Hull.

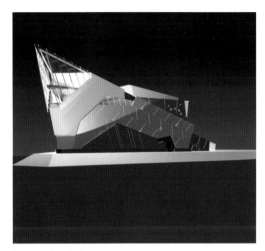

Perspective from the River Humber.

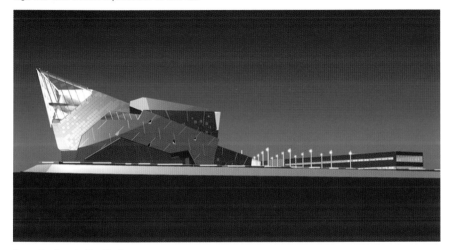

Perspectives from the River Humber.

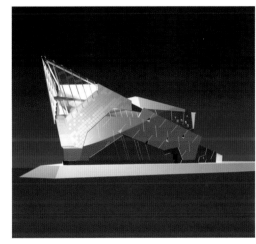

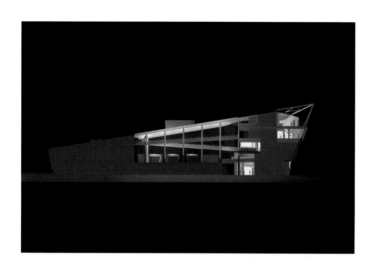
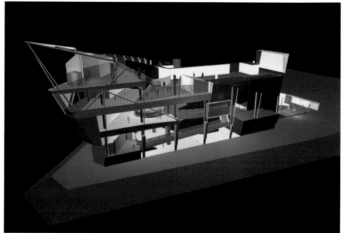
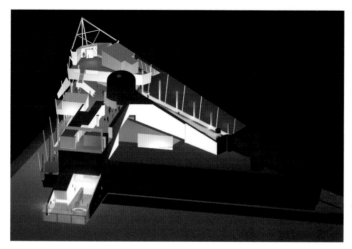
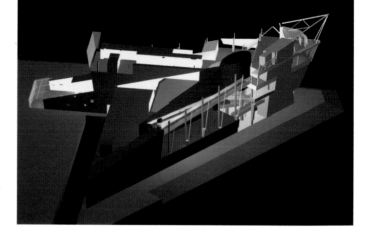

Computer model exploring spatial arrangement.

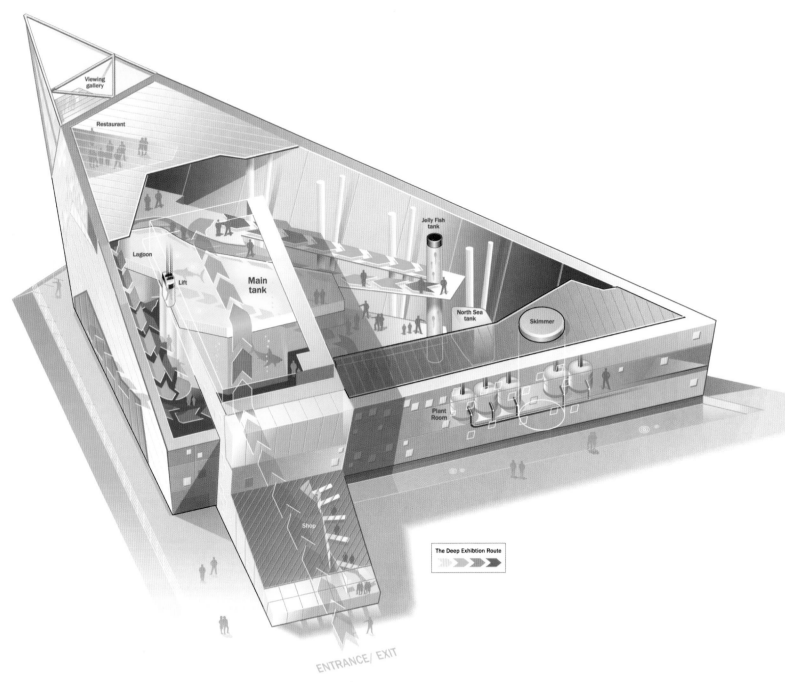

Viewing gallery

Restaurant

Lagoon

Lift

Main tank

Jelly Fish tank

North Sea tank

Skimmer

Plant Room

Shop

The Deep Exhibtion Route

ENTRANCE/ EXIT

Circulation route takes visitors to the top of the building where they begin their journey down to the deep.

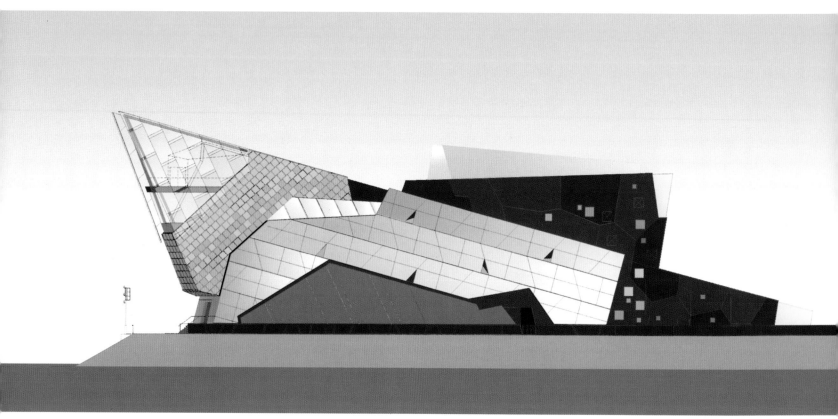

South elevation.

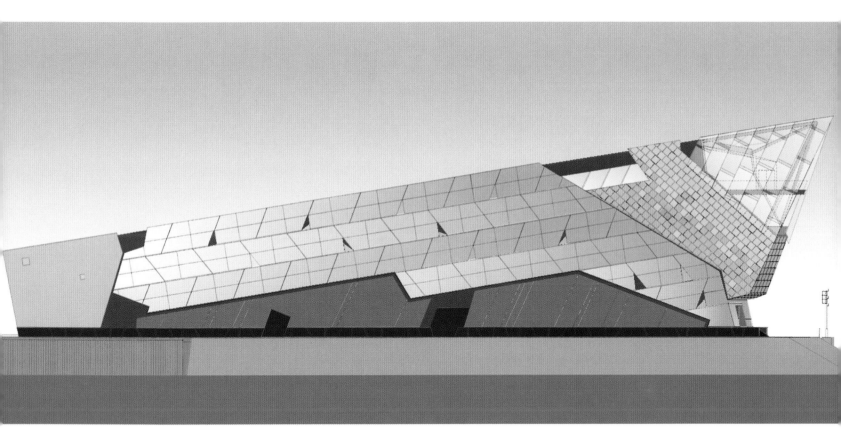

West elevation.

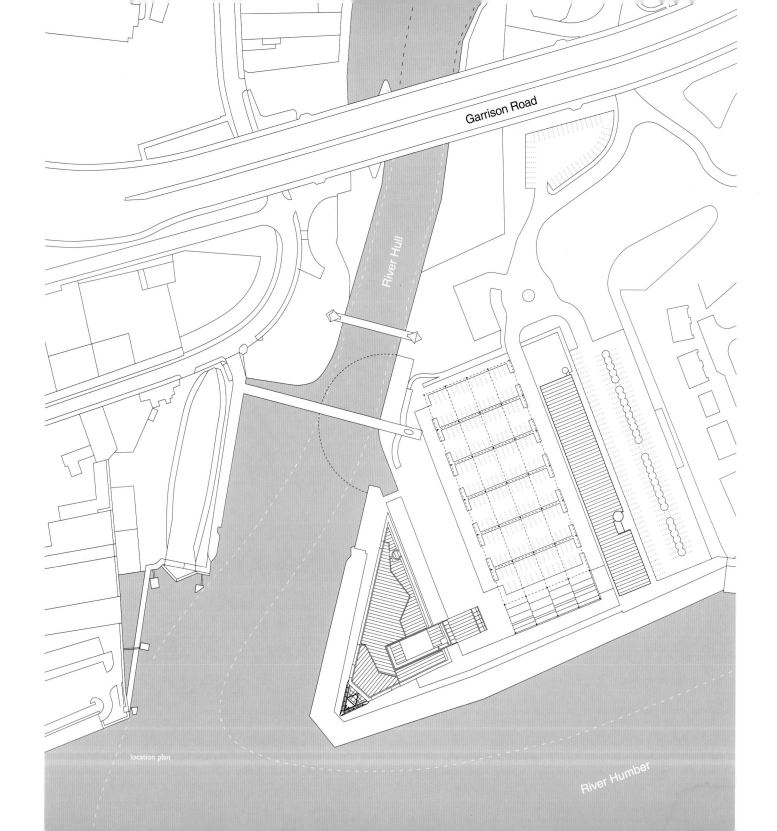

Garrison Road

River Hull

location plan

River Humber

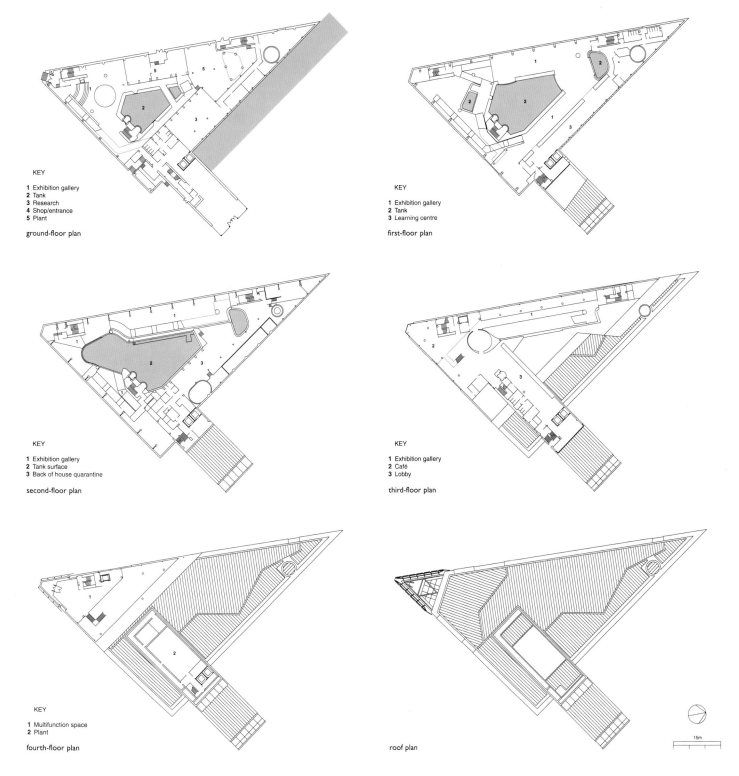

KEY

1 Exhibition gallery
2 Tank
3 Research
4 Shop/entrance
5 Plant

ground-floor plan

KEY

1 Exhibition gallery
2 Tank
3 Learning centre

first-floor plan

KEY

1 Exhibition gallery
2 Tank surface
3 Back of house quarantine

second-floor plan

KEY

1 Exhibition gallery
2 Café
3 Lobby

third-floor plan

KEY

1 Multifunction space
2 Plant

fourth-floor plan

roof plan

15m

UNDERGROUND AND OVERGROUND: BUILDING

There is not a duplicate piece of steel on the job – around 1700 or 1800 members, each of which is different.

Richard Dean, Bovis Lend Lease

THE DEEP

Building The Deep

Farrell's decision to push The Deep right to the edge of the Humber repeated the practice of previous generations of builders here. From the time of Henry VIII onwards, the aim was always to defend the city right on the water's edge at the confluence of the two rivers. However, an important topographical change had taken place in the 19th century. The building of inland docks affected the tidal movement of water, and existing mudflats began to silt up more rapidly. Effectively, the point began to extend itself southwards into the Humber, beyond the original edge.

In the expansionist shipbuilding days of the mid to late 19th century, this land was reclaimed to become "Sammy's Point", which meant that, by putting the new building at the southern edge on this relatively new land, important archaeological remains from earlier times were left relatively undisturbed.

The fortifications of Henry VIII had been subsumed into the great Citadel, covering 30 acres. The southernmost point of this great defensive complex, known as the southern blockhouse, was levelled along with the rest of the Citadel once it had ceased to be militarily important in the 1860s. Industry took over the site. However, the extensive foundations of the Citadel and its Tudor antecedent still exist, starting with the southern blockhouse immediately to the north of The Deep, then continuing under the busy 1980s relief road and out the other side.

Following archaeological investigations from the late 1980s, much was known about the position and extent of this scheduled ancient monument, and so the layout and approach to The Deep was considered with a view to what lay beneath the ground. However, the clearing of the site offered the opportunity for further digs. One superlative find from the consequent dig of 1997 was a great Tudor cannon – a "port piece" of Henry VIII's day, contemporary with his doomed warship the Mary Rose. Very few examples of this type exist. And whereas the guns on that ill-fated ship had largely corroded away in sea water, here it was found to be in good condition. Records dating back to 1547 list it as Henry's property, so it was identifiable immediately upon being discovered. As an obsolete Tudor weapon, it had been buried in the foundations of the later Citadel, probably in 1681 – there may well be more such armaments waiting to be found there. This impressive 4m long example of heavy artillery, known simply as "Henry's Gun", today forms the centrepiece of Hull's newly-expanded and improved museum quarter in the nearby High Street, just over the River Hull from The Deep. As city archaeologist Martin Foreman writes about the importance of the find: "Its provenance underlines the historic status of east bank sites. It thereby assists the unified presentation of the historic urban core."

Erection of steelwork, March 2000.

The site before work commenced.

Since The Deep was erected on 19th century reclaimed land, there was little of archaeological interest to be found in the ground there apart from some "dolphins" – heavy timber mooring posts sunk into the water's edge to help sailing ships manoeuvre round into the haven of the River Hull. There were also some 19th century industrial remains, including iron pipes thought to be part of an early steam-powered hydraulic system installed here, and which provided power to much of the industry of east Hull. The approaches to The Deep, however, had to tread carefully since they traversed ancient ground. Thus the approach road was designed to sweep round the underground presence of the southern blockhouse so that its remnants – which are in an excellent state of preservation – might be revealed at a later date. As the regeneration of this part of the city quickens, it is likely that the presence of more and more of the lost Citadel – a stupendous structure for its time –

will become increasingly apparent. The arrival of the new building has thus helped to further understanding of the rich history of the area.

Interestingly, it appears that the Citadel, like Farrell's 21st century building, presented very different elevations on its three sides and was most dominant when viewed from the city it was meant to protect. This is not unconnected with Hull's famous independence of spirit and sometimes muted loyalty to the Crown down the centuries. Both Henry VIII and Charles II regarded the city as a potential hotbed of rebellion: domestic dissent was as real a threat as foreign invasion.

However, the preparation of the site had to contend with more than archeological remains. First it had to be cleared of the toxic waste associated with its former industrial uses: fortunately, it was found to be not too badly contaminated, with only one or two "hot spots" needing to be dealt with.

May 2000. Roof of Business Centre nears completion.

June 2000. Steelwork is erected around main tank.

Cladding begins on the east elevation.

January 2001. Erection of cladding begins.

As for the ground conditions encountered on the building site proper, that was typical shoreline silt – much the same as the builders of the old fortifications had had to cope with. In their case they used timber piles. The Deep deployed 30-metre long concrete piles that pass through the silt and alluvium to bed down in an underlying layer of clay and gravel.

Once the land had been cleared, the chosen management contractor for the job in May 1999 was Bovis Lend Lease. Piling began in October that year. For site manager, Bovis appointed Richard Dean, who had previously worked on another unique building complex, Sir Michael Hopkins' Jubilee Campus at Nottingham University. "I had acquired a taste for imaginative projects," says Dean. "Working with these people, you know it's going to be interesting. So I was lucky enough to move from the Nottingham job onto The Deep in Hull."

This was the first aquarium-based project Bovis had ever done in the UK, so they tapped into their expertise in this area in the USA: useful, as it turned out, since the key contractor for the massively thick acrylic walls to the tanks was to be an American company, Reynolds Polymer of Grand Junction, Colorado. Reynolds' consultancy arm, ICM, advised Farrell on the constructional elements of the aquaria.

The work was arranged with Farrell's office as design team leaders and contract administrators, Bovis as management contractor, and BDP as project managers on behalf of the client. Farrell in turn organised the structural and services engineering consultancies, exhibition and landscape design, while Bovis organised the construction work into 29 packages which were then let out to the various contractors. The amicable professional relationship between Dean and Farrell's project architect Darren Cartlidge was to prove important to the running of the project, not least because they were of similar age and outlook, and even both found themselves becoming fathers, in each case twice, within months of each other during the three-year progress of the works. This relationship was then nurtured in the Farrell on-site team of Moz Hussain, Karl James and Mike Barry, who worked alongside the Bovis team.

Also key to the final public impact of The Deep – because of the way building and content was always seen as indivisible – was the architects' relationship with exhibition designers, John Csáky Associates Ltd. This was a big contract in itself, and Csáky's team alone numbered six – him as project director, Andrew Wood-Walker as senior designer, Mat Mason as senior graphic designer, Catherine Hall as storyline co-ordinator, Jason Hender as technical and site supervisor, and Avril Levack as project administrator. Csáky recalls how, in early discussions with the architects, the structure of the building was designed to accommodate his ideas for the display. "We were particularly pleased that the spacing of

January 2001.

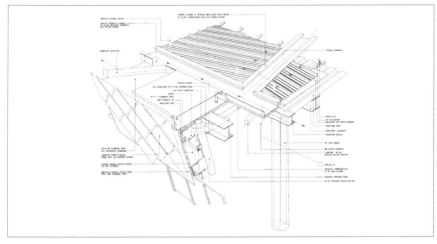

Black waterproof layer of cladding system prior to erection of marine-grade aluminium panels.

Roof and wall cladding construction detail.

the main structural columns was adjusted to align them with the landings on the long ramps down, so that we could attach plasma screens and interactive exhibits at a point where the visitor would naturally pause and engage with the storyline. This is an excellent example of a proper integration of the detailed storyline with the building – of architects and exhibition designers working well together."

From a constructional point of view, however, the first task was the creation of the central concrete structure to house the display tanks. This was built first, and then the rest of The Deep was assembled around it in the form of a steel frame. Work on the central aquarium elements, from building the tank through to specialist fit-out of the underwater "scenery" and final purification and stocking with fish, followed a separate critical path throughout from the rest of the building, almost as if they were two distinct buildings, one contained inside the other. Towards the end, conventional building workers found themselves working alongside Danish seascape contractors Pangea Rocks – essentially commercial sculptors – who installed the amazingly realistic coral reefs.

This apparently neat separation of tank structure and surrounding building did not make everything simple. Because of the unique shape of The Deep, repetition of elements did not play much of a part. "There is not a duplicate piece of steel on the job

– around 1700 or 1800 members, each of which is different," as Dean puts it. The builders had to know exactly what they were doing, unlike on a conventional rectilinear steel-frame building where one column or beam is much the same as another. A further element was the need to include a 1.2m high tidal flood defence into the scheme. Sited downstream of the River Hull tidal surge barrier and consequently enjoying no flood protection, the building had to be detailed in such a way that water could lap high all round it without entering and damaging it. This is subtly done: effectively the whole building sits on a shallow in-situ concrete tank, with all openings placed above the calculated high-water mark in the event of such a flood. True to the layered aesthetic of the building, this concrete skirt is exposed and exploited, moulded into angled and coloured striations as part of the overall tectonic design of the exterior.

Planning such a complicated construction job was far from conventional. Apart from the complexity of the steelwork, for instance, the transparent acrylic walls for the tanks and in-tank lift shaft were on a 12-month lead-in time that could have delayed the whole project. Large sections of the roof had to be left off so that acrylic sections weighing six and eight tonnes could be dropped in later in the construction process. The roof skin itself was unconventional,

being highly visible from the elevated road nearby and designed, like the elevations, with a "tectonic" aesthetic requiring the metal roofing to be laid in contrasting sections. All the normal hitches and glitches during the overall construction process were encountered but the only one to have a big impact on the programme was the celebrated design rethink of Christmas 1999, when the cladding was redesigned and re-engineered, and the siting of the aquarium life-support systems was moved into the building from its previous remote location.

This was by no means mere detail. "Before Christmas that year we knew it was all about to happen, and we came back after Christmas to new elevations," as Dean puts it. The main cladding module, for instance, halved in size. Previously the idea was to have giant (8m x 4m) stainless steel panels, each weighing around six tonnes. This changed to 4m x 2m marine-grade aluminium panels, the largest available in that material. The mounting of the cladding had to be thought through from scratch, and considerable alterations were also needed to the structural frame of the building. The cladding and frame contractors, Mero UK, played a large part in the redesign, working with Farrell's cladding specialist Jason Speechly-Dick and Bovis. There was an intense eight-week redesign period, with the cladding being developed as the frame was being built, and the

View from Albert Dock.

Glazed observatory.

Aerial view, March 2002.

glazing package then being rolled into the cladding contract. The result is impressive: the built elevations exactly mirror the Farrell artwork.

This was not quite the way Antoni Gaudi used to build in Spain: the eccentric Catalonian genius was quite capable of treating real buildings like working models, tearing down already-built elements in order to accommodate later design changes. No, things were not at that stage. However, it was a worrying time: how much delay would the changes cause in a tight programme? Without careful rethinking, there could have been an unwelcome hiatus in construction. But judicious juggling of the design elements meant that construction could continue in parallel with design. The smaller, lighter cladding panels were also easier to manoeuvre into position in this windy, exposed site, and could be adjusted to tighter tolerances. In the end, Dean reckons that around 16 weeks were added to the construction programme as a result of the big redesign, against which there were cost savings made by taking the aquarium life support systems into the main building, which also made the systems much more user-friendly.

"There's no doubt it was a painful thing to have to do," concludes Dean now, "but I think the building is twice what it would have been. At the end of the day, it's a stunning building. Which is the reason I got involved with it in the first place."

Cladding details.

Facts and figures

- The building used 800 tonnes of structural steel

- Its external machine-cut aluminium panels are the largest possible in the UK

- They form the first use of a marine-grade aluminium rainscreen system in the UK, assembled to a tiny tolerance of 1.5mm

- 18,000 rivets and 12,000 specialist screws fixed the black aluminium sub-façade

- The Deep's outer walls lean at 8 and 15 degrees

- Its nose cone is the longest elliptical tube structure in the UK

- The building is designed to withstand tidal surges and 100mph hurricanes

- It has the deepest aquarium tank in Europe at 10 metres

- The main tank is one of the biggest in Europe

- Total amount of water at any one time in the building is 2,850,000 litres (627,000 gallons) weighing 2,850 tonnes

- It takes 87 tonnes of salt to be mixed into the water of the main tank

- The aquarium mixes its own salt water in specially designed tanks

- The "skimmer tower" which purifies the water is the world's largest, with a capacity of 1,500 cubic metres an hour

- The Deep has the deepest underwater acrylic tunnel in Europe

- It has the first ever glazed lift to rise through an aquarium tank

- It includes the largest "total environment simulator" in Europe, operated by the University of Hull, which simulates estuarial tidal flow and sediments

- Viewing platforms are 24m above sea level

- It cost £45.5m and took three years to build on 29 separate Works Contract packages

OMPLETING THE DEEP

So often in life, the reality turns out to be less than the dream. With the birth of The Deep, however, we saw the birth of something new and unique. The fusion of the building with its story, of interactives with aquaria and commerce with leisure, turned out to be much more than we had allowed ourselves to imagine, back at the beginning.

Colin Brown, Chief Executive, The Deep

The Deep in context with the city of Hull viewed from the south bank of the River Humber.

Completing The Deep

As the designers and contractors moved towards the completion of the project, things were comparatively relaxed. True, the opening date had originally been meant to be earlier, but people always tend to work up to deadlines, and this particular deadline was set for March 23rd 2002, the start of the Easter holidays. A month prior to that – a time when many such new visitor attractions tend to find themselves running worryingly late, with substantial work needing to be done right up to, and even after, public opening – only finishing-off work and the final landscaping outside remained to be done, with one exception – the steel pedestrian swing bridge intended to connect The Deep across the mouth of the River Hull to the Victoria Pier area, thus stitching together the historic quarter and completing a substantial length of car-free riverside walkway, was not in place. A relatively simple, functional structure by The Deep's structural engineers Jubb and Partners, with Bennett Associated engineers, it had been made on the other side of the estuary in Barrow on Humber, and delivered on time. But its installation was delayed by an unexpected dispute over the necessary clearance for boats making the turn from the Humber into the Hull. Like the Tate Modern in London, though for rather different reasons, The Deep opened without its pedestrian bridge operational: though it was sitting there on dry land for all to see. The installation delay was forecast to be around six months as one of the approach piles in the river was moved and the bridge extended some three metres to compensate.

That little irritation aside – plus the ironically late arrival of a school of North Sea cod, which proved more difficult to track down than hammerhead sharks – the auguries were good. With some very positive national media coverage leading up to the opening, it was clear that The Deep had succeeded in its mission of being regarded as a cultural building rather than as just another fish zoo of the kind that is handled perfectly adequately by commercial companies. Arts critics, as much as science reporters and travel writers, were on the case. Photographer Richard Bryant's glowing images of the building, capturing the quicksilver interrelationship of architecture, water and sky, were attracting attention from as far afield as Tokyo. Even London-based BBC producers started making unprecedented enquiries about the unfamiliar journey to Hull.

One worry had been removed with the successful opening of the Magna Science Centre in Rotherham, in 2001. The jinx on Yorkshire's new Lottery-funded visitor attractions had finally been lifted. Following the failure of the first incarnation of the Earth Centre in Doncaster, and the closure of the National Rock and Pop Museum in Sheffield, there had been fears that Magna – an ambitious concept to introduce to a town not known as a

South elevation viewed from the promenade.

Detail showing pearlescent back-enamelled glass tiles.

visitor destination – would go the same way. Far from it. Visitor numbers at Magna were substantially higher than anticipated. This was good in some ways, bad in others since heavy physical wear and tear on the interactive equipment had led to frequent breakdowns of the displays.

Of course, one does not really know the true success or otherwise of such places until time has passed, the initial novelty has worn off, and the task of creating a loyal following of returning visitors has been achieved. Even so, Colin Brown, The Deep's director, and Councillor David Gemmell had cautiously insisted on the break-even visitor number figure being held down to around the 200,000 a year mark. The displays were designed to be tough and durable. Giant aquarium tanks are hard to break. Most of the interactives took the form of computer touch-screens (though as Brown remarked, touch-screens can too easily become punch-screens) while

the physical interactives were robustly made.

Round about this time, Brown did test-runs of The Deep with parties of schoolchildren and received an enthusiastic response, though perhaps a truer test, because it was unexpected, came when three families arrived at the building from some distance away, expecting it to be already open. Rather than disappoint them, Brown personally showed them round the unfinished building and found himself basking in unforced praise. Given that school bookings were by then solid, that advance corporate bookings were coming in from as far afield as the West Country, that the separate business centre was proving a commercial success and that the local press and population was taking a fierce pride in the building, it was beginning to seem unlikely that The Deep would fall flat on its pointy face.

Brown even audaciously set up good-value package deals with independent operator Hull Trains,

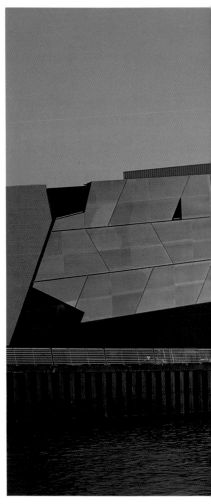

North elevation.

West elevation.

View from River Hull.

View from observation deck to Humber Bridge.

offering direct trips with inclusive hotel to Londoners, plus similar deals with North Sea Ferries to attract Dutch and Belgian tourists. That really will be one to watch: if cultural tourists nationally and internationally as well as regionally were to start regarding Hull as a destination, then Brown and Gemmell would finally have succeeded in the tourism aims they set for the city all those years ago. But that will be a gradual process, and may well depend on other urban improvements being carried out as prompted by Farrell's Hull 2020 masterplan. Relatively remote Hull in East Yorkshire, unlike the cheek-by-jowl cities of South Yorkshire, does not have a very large population within a few miles. To go there, people have to show commitment.

That has always been the gamble of The Deep. Could Sir Terry Farrell's building do for the city at least some of what Sir Nicholas Grimshaw's wildly successful Eden Project, which like Magna opened in 2001, did for far-flung mid-Cornwall? The catch is that people go to Cornwall for their holidays anyway. In contrast, tourists – in particular family tourists – to the predominantly rural East Riding of Yorkshire have in the past tended to avoid Hull. Now, there is a good reason to go there. The Deep is the first real top-notch family attraction the city has ever had. But forecasting visitor numbers is like conducting political opinion polls: when the real poll comes along, there is always the potential for surprise, one way or the other. The official line remained steadfastly conservative: a requirement of just 200,000 annual visitors, with the main catchment being a two-hour drive from Hull. But Brown became noticeably more confident as the opening date neared and the media reviews started to roll in. "It's clear we are now being associated with the best in the world," he said shortly before launch day. "Our aspirations have grown with the project." By Easter weekend, a week after the opening, The Deep had taken 55,000 visitors, equating to 23 per cent of its business plan for the entire year. By the end of its first operating quarter, visitors numbered 250,000.

What visitors find is a building of national and even international status as a piece of architecture, and which happens to have over 2,800 marine creatures living in it. Apart from the landscaping around the building itself, some important landscape improvements were made to the pedestrian links with the raised relief road bridge running a little way north of the site – since, until the new pedestrian bridge opened, this somewhat exposed and noisy route formed the nearest connection by foot with the city centre. It is very clear that The Deep is a regeneration pioneer in this part of town, colonising what was previously a forgotten area and making a link between the old city and the previously isolated big new housing development further east on what had been Victoria Dock. The next stage will clearly

View from observation deck to Holy Trinity Church.

The water reflects on to the angled surface of the nose cone.

The building is seemingly suspended over the waterfront and landmarks the joining of the rivers Humber and Hull.

Cladding detail expressing TFP's fissure analogy.

be the extension of this prototype cultural quarter northwards up the River Hull corridor, revealing as it goes the huge hidden extent of the archaeological remains of the Citadel and its Tudor predecessor. In the meantime, getting to the place remains slightly challenging.

The building itself has a range of activities beyond its primary purpose as a visitor attraction. The business centre provides serviced offices and laboratories for start-up firms, especially those related to marine industries. It is a cleanly-detailed, no-nonsense long two-storey rectangular block, forming an inhabited wall towards the eastern edge of the site, with its own dedicated car parking concealed behind. This is by no means a small building, with a gross floor area of 3,300 sq m compared with the 7,200 sq m of the main building. A mosaic-clad drum marks the glazed double-height entrance, while inside are all the facilities you might expect from a modern, high-specification "Incubator" office building. The commercial success of the Business Centre, with extra space becoming free once the design teams had moved out of their big temporary office at the end of the building, proved vital to the financial equation of The Deep.

Just as important to the overall mix is The Deep Research Facility, run by the University of Hull. This, which occupies a chunk of the main building at ground level, is both site-related and global in its work on water and silt movement: a seemingly hermetic specialist activity that is rendered spectacular by the facility's Total Environment Simulator, also known as the Research Flume. Essentially, complete coastal, estuarine and river environments can be recreated in miniature in the 16m long, 6m wide and 1.6m deep flume. When loaded up in use, this chunk of equipment weighs 200 tonnes. It can generate its own currents and waves, tropical rainstorms and the like. The University has links with many other marine research departments around the world, and visiting academics will form a further layer of regular visitors to The Deep. The Research Facility provides the necessary gravitas to the more immediately accessible attractions of The Deep, and reinforces the point that the educational mission of the project works at several levels.

But the key to the greater or lesser success of The Deep will be largely determined by its impact as a physical object. All its contents could be placed in a low-cost warehouse on a quayside somewhere, but then very few people outside the immediate area would bother to visit. What makes the building different is twofold. First is its appearance as a stylized geological outcrop, enriched with secondary metaphors: you can see in it, if you choose, the form of a leaping fish, complete with scales, or a marine crustacean. This external appearance, on two of

Detail of 'punched' windows to entrance tower.

its sides, contrives to disguise completely the fact that much of this building is, as it must be (and as most modern art galleries and museums are), a windowless exhibition space. The rich layering of the façades, which exercised the design team so greatly in the early stages, entirely compensates for this inward-looking nature. It is an old architectural game, played at a high level.

Secondly, the architecture is not skin-deep. It runs through to the bone. The whole arrangement of the interior, especially the disposition of ramps and platforms making up the exhibition route around the great central tank, governs and is governed by the strong concept of the exhibition it contains. The building is as much a part of that exhibition as the fish or the computer screens. It works in both a linear and volumetric fashion to achieve its effects. It avoids design clichés, be they the lure of the exquisite detail or the distractingly sculptural interior

space. You are not especially aware, for instance, of the nature of the handrails or floor finishes. They are good, but they are not the point. The fetishising of materials, deployed so successfully on the exterior, is held firmly in check in the interior where there are other things to look at.

And finally, the building is of its context. An odd thing to say, perhaps, given its uniquely eye-catching properties, but this is the case nonetheless. The shape and history of the site helped to generate the form of the building just as much as its role as a vessel of metaphor. It is a tough building in tough surroundings. It understands and works with the huge flat seascapes and skyscapes and the nature of the estuarial light. It also provides an excellent vantage-point for the city without resorting to observation-deck platitudes.

'Hokey-cokey' windows to east elevation.

The Deep at the mouth of the River Hull

The promenade lighting augments the illumination of the façade.

View of observation deck and restaurant viewing point below.

The Deep in the context of its waterfront surrounds.

Entrance tower glazed gallery.

Business Centre entrance.

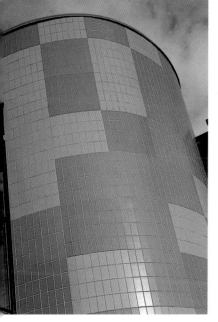

Stair tower.

Detail of rendered elevation.

INSIDE THE DEEP:
WHAT

YOU SEE

The Deep represents the newest, most exciting development of the public aquaria genre. The innovative integration of cutting-edge audio-visual presentation, stunning aquaria and a sincere wish to increase awareness of the story and current plight of the world's oceans make this a must-see attraction.

Dr. David Gibson, Director of Husbandry & Operations

Inside The Deep

When you arrive at the top of the building and take in the first of the framed views of the surrounding land and waterscape, you are at the start of the exhibition: also at the start of a journey. This is a physical journey, in that it takes you gently right back down through the building before shooting you upwards back to the top, in rather more spectacular fashion than your arrival. It is also, however, a journey through time and into depth. Not for nothing is The Deep so named.

Your route is not timed – you are free to wander through at your leisure. Being a linear route descending through the building, generated by the building's architecture, it is intended to be self-policing. On quiet days there will be time to linger in the set-piece areas. At busy times the increased pressure of people ought naturally to encourage people to move through faster. The trick of the circulation pattern is that you arrive back at your starting point on the third floor where there is a café and viewing platform: so nothing is missed.

The overall concept of the exhibition is that it should transport you from the dawn of time, represented by the 'Big Bang' origin of the Universe – through the oceans of past, present and future. The future is represented by a notional deep-ocean research station, Deep Blue One, placed appropriately enough right at the bottom of the building. Thanks to the arts of architect and exhibition designer, it feels as if it is set at a much greater depth than is actually the case. Partly this is because of the physical layout of the building – you glimpse lower levels in such a way as to make them seem a very long way down, and they are lit so as to help this illusion – and partly because of the sense of depth engendered by your glimpses into the undersea world of the big aquarium tanks, at various stages of your progress. Descending past that great weight of living water gives a sense almost of compression.

The message of the building's architecture – that the story of the oceans is also the story of geology, so setting up a fruitful dialogue between solid and liquid, rock and water – is carried through in the exhibition. After a preamble in the "myths and legends" gallery, invoking many of the old stories of the mysteries of the seas, with words from explorer Christopher Columbus, Shakespeare's *Tempest*, Coleridge's *Rime of the Ancient Mariner* and so forth, you pass through the turnstiles into the real world of today, which is even more strange. A tank ahead of you displays some of the weirdest living sea creatures to be found – longhorned cowfish, warty frogfish, Chinese trumpetfish, batfish, curious-looking aquatic beast of all kinds. Then you move into a small, dark rotunda that, like a mini-planetarium, gives you the Big Bang, in shimmering fibre-optics, computer animation, multi-media projection and sound.

Restaurant level.

Window to 'Endless Ocean'.

'Northern Seas' zone.

'Lagoon of Light'.

The 'Endless Ocean' zone.

The 'Awakening Seas' zone.

The birth of matter takes place in a dazzling flash and shoots towards you. The universe is re-created once every 90 seconds.

From here, you emerge into the first of the big spaces, at the top of the ramp that will gradually lead you down and round the building, like an angular Guggenheim. You are in the "awakening seas" section, covering the evolution of the oceans from their creation as the Earth cooled and continents were formed, to the birth of life. At intervals, plasma screens, localised sound-domes and interactive devices for adults and children further explain the story. The timescale is graphically demonstrated: every 1.5 centimetres of the handrail on your descent represents a million years of elapsed time. And what you encounter first is not water, but rock: the impressive 10 metre high "fossil wall" that dominates the opening sequences. This is a cunningly-made bit of scenery, the idea being that a section of rockface has fallen or eroded away to reveal the fossilized remains of all kinds of ancient sea creatures.

As you move towards this, there is still no hint of the huge aquaria to come, although you encounter a preliminary cylindrical tank at the point where the ramp cranks back on itself past the fossil wall. Here you find jellyfish, representative of the primitive organisms that colonised the early oceans. The next leg, as you pass directly beneath the fossil wall, moves into the evolution of sea creatures with backbones,

with all that means in terms of speed and manoeuvrability. This section concludes with the arrival of mammals and, finally, 30,000 years ago, humans. "We equate the depth that different animals can get to in the oceans, with the machines that man has created to get to those depths himself," explains Dr. David Gibson, curator of the exhibition. Which is why, from here, you move into the zones with the big tanks.

The space widens out, and you are gazing across a clear-walled lagoon – tropical shallows, a coral atoll in the Caribbean or Pacific – at the start of a journey through the present-day oceans. Computer-interactive screens all around help you to identify the species. The lagoon merges with the top of the deep tank beyond, looking towards the quarantine and husbandry area. To the other side of this space is the "discovery tank", a low rocky pool where visitors can get to grips with some real marine life.

From here you plunge deeper into the coral seas, looking at living coral and at displays concerning the importance of coral to the eco-systems of the oceans. The artificial corals in the deep tank, built by the Danish firm Pangea Rocks, are remarkably realistic, and seem to fool even the fish. Gathering the fish was a lengthy process in itself. They come from sustainable sources, mainly Fiji and Florida, inspected personally by Dr. Gibson. There are 118 different species, and more than 2,800 individuals in all.

Mandarin fish.

Box fish.

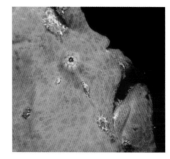

Warty Frog fish.

Nurse Shark and Golden Trevally in the 'Endless Oceans' tank.

Coral shelf leading to 'Endless Oceans' with Nurse Shark in the foreground.

DB-1 ARCHIVE SEQUENCE
PLAY MODE

Views of Deep Blue One.

Up at the quarantine and husbandry area are other tanks, ones you don't see unless you get a special behind-the-scenes tour: the one they mix the salt water in (for it is manufactured on site to exactly the right level of pollution-free purity), holding tanks for salt and fresh water, and (towards the rear of the building) the cylindrical concrete protein skimmer tower which keeps the water optically clear. Staff access to the surface of the main display tanks is also done from up here: there's even a small rowing-boat kept standing by.

Soon, you get your first glimpse into the big tank – the Open Seas section – with its scores of species, and – though you are just beneath the surface at this point – you start to get a physical idea of the central concept of depth. Looking through the huge acrylic viewing panel, or sticking your head up into the underwater viewing domes, and especially trying out the periscope, is to feel a little like Jules Verne's Captain Nemo from his prophetic 1870 novel *Twenty Thousand Leagues Under the Sea*. Nemo's marvellous submarine Nautilus boasted huge panoramic windows, allowing the wildlife of the oceans to be observed at close quarters. Later, some of this became reality in the televised 1960s and 1970s underwater exploits of Jacques Cousteau, which apart from being popular television proved mightily influential on a new generation of marine biologists –

Coral wall.

Tuba diver launches BBC Music Live event.

'Lagoon of Light' with Bonnethead Shark.

Dr. Gibson diving in 'Endless Oceans'.

The Deep's Dr. David Gibson among them – and which achieved a kind of apotheosis with David Attenborough's 2001 TV series The Blue Planet. Much of the technology and interpretation available to that series – which means the resources of marine institutes around the world – is deployed at The Deep.

Here you might get a glimpse not only of sharks and rays, but also such oddities as the huge, slightly unnerving Potato Cod, which sounds like it wants to be a convenience food: fish and chips combined. But it is a tropical fish: the cod we associate with food are still to come, in the North Sea tank.

The next glimpse into the undersea world, as you round the corner, marks the transition from shallow to deep, where the coral shelves away into the open ocean. There is a magnitude change in the creatures inhabiting these regions: big Napoleon wrasse, white-tipped reef sharks, Golden Trevally and suchlike. This is the introduction to the section known as "Endless Oceans", and contains smaller, special-interest tanks around the edges of your route. These concentrate on specific aspects of the biology of fishes, such as cleaning, symbiotic relationships, camouflage, predatory and defence mechanisms. All are supported by interactive computer screens.

Beyond that section, the space opens up again and two big aquaria face each other – another great curved window into the big Pacific tank faces the North Sea Tank. There you find not the exotic species, but the fish that you'd more normally see on a fishmonger's slab, swimming around au naturel in a seascape that is – as so much of the North Sea is – industrial, with a pipeline running through it. It is telling that Gibson had some difficulty tracking down large enough cod (eventually the fish came from farmed sources). Cod can grow huge, but over-fishing means that as the stock dwindles, the individuals caught get steadily younger and smaller. Man's interaction with the oceans is as important to the story as the unspoilt tropical paradises beloved of the TV programme-makers.

From here you make a turn through a cavern, the "Kingdom of Ice", complete with its real frozen sections of wall to bring the temperature right down. Which leads naturally enough to an interactive section dealing with global warming and the effects of rising seas on various parts of the world – locally, in the Humber Estuary, then on a European and finally on a global level.

There is an education room up here in the corner of the building, fitted out for schools and subdivisible into separate areas depending on how many schools are in and what's on the agenda. But if you're not in a school party, you'll continue straight on down to the climax of the show: the undersea research station dubbed Deep Blue One. Big screens show the images received from your voyage in the virtual ocean depths – the idea being that you are plunging deep into a realm rarely glimpsed by humans. Solid display objects also find their place in this atmospheric, sci-fi environment, such as a replica "Black Smoker", an example of the volcanic vents at the foot of the deepest ocean trenches. It's part laboratory, part vessel, part information display, with the agreeable fiction being maintained that live input is being received from a number of other similar oceanographic stations around the world. You can even sit in submarine training simulators.

The final trick is still to be played. After leaving Deep Blue One, you are in the tail end of the exhibition – even the computers that power all the displays are put on view – and you might normally expect to be ushered to the exit. Not so here, or not in the usual way. From the low-key final section called "Reflections", dealing with the way the media portrays the marine environment – you suddenly dive through a transparent tunnel at the bottom of the main tank – at 10 metres down, the deepest such viewing passage in the world. Fish swim above your head, the silhouettes of sharks outlined against the light from above. Emerging from the tunnel, you arrive at a scenic lift in its own clear tunnel which whisks you up through the tank, out through the surface of the water, and thus back to the start: the café, the mezzanine floor above that, and the viewing gallery in the nosecone of the building, looking back

over Hull and beyond that, framing the Humber Bridge in the middle distance.

To exit, it's down in the conventional lifts and out past the shop in the entrance wing. Though at times, there will also be public access to Hull University's specialist Total Environment Simulator at ground level, where the ebb and flow of tides and movement of land in estuarial settings will be created in test tanks.

Tank statistics

Endless Oceans: 2.3m litres, 10 metres deep, 25m x 15m wide (average) with acrylic tunnel and lift ride and viewing domes

Lagoon: 200,000 litres, 1.2m deep, coral wall 3.5m deep

North Sea: 200,000 litres, 5m deep, 10m wide

Polar: 2.4m long, 1.2m deep

Discovery pool: 4m long, 0.5m deep

Reef tank: 3,600 litres, 4m long, 0.5m deep

Jellyfish tank: 3,510 litres, 2m high, 1.5m diameter

"Jewel" tanks: five tanks of 1 cubic metre

The fish: 118 different species, over 2,800 individuals

Corals in the 'Lagoon of Light'.

Nurse Shark and Golden Trevally in 'Endless Oceans'.

The completion and opening of The Deep marked the end of one long process and the start of another: the next phase in the revival of Kingston upon Hull. It worked immediately in one very important sense: it got people talking about the city. The image of The Deep started to be associated with Hull. A background place for so long, a name with few beneficial contemporary associations, Hull has gained a powerful three-dimensional identifier.

Iconic image at sunset.

SPONSORS
& CO

CREDITS

NSULTANTS

Sponsors

Partners
The Deep is a partnership between Kingston upon Hull City Council and the University of Hull.

Funders and supporters
The Millennium Commission

European Regional Development Fund

Yorkshire Forward (the local Regional Development Agency)

The Single Regeneration Budget via Hull City Vision Ltd

National Australia Bank

Garfield Weston Foundation

National Westminster Bank

Environment Agency

Fishmongers Guild

Consultants

Project client
EMIH Limited ('The Deep')

Client agent
John Dixon

Operational client
Running Deep Ltd

Architect, lead design consultant, contract administrator
Terry Farrell & Partners

Management contractor
Bovis Lend Lease Ltd

Project manager
Building Design Partnership

Exhibition design
John Csáky Associates

Structural engineer
Jubb and Partners

Services engineer, fire consultant, acoustic engineer
Waterman Gore

Quantity surveyor
Gleeds

Exhibition quantity surveyor
Walfords

Planning supervisor
Brown Smith Baker

Landscape architect
Casella Stanger

Tank fit-out/ seascaping designs
International Concept Management

Life support systems for Aquarium tanks
Intensive Aquaculture Technology

Specialist lighting design
DHA Design Services Ltd

Hospitality consultants
RGA

Contractors

Aquarium Technology

Atacama

NG Bailey & Co Ltd

Berkeley Projects UK Ltd

Boningale

Clark Construction

Electrosonic

Goresline Surveying

Hewlett Civil Engineering Ltd

Heyrods Construction Ltd

Intensive Aquaculture Technology

Irvine Whitlock

JW Taylor Ltd

Kingston Communications Plc

Kvaerner Construction

LM Engineering

Mero (UK) Plc

Otis Ltd

Pangea Rocks aps

Red Group Omega

Reynolds Polymer

Scenic Route

SIAC Construction (UK) Ltd

Transco

Wescol & Glosford/Bison

Yorkshire Electricity

Yorkshire Water

Team credits

Client team
The Deep

Colin Brown
Tom Bellringer
Freya Cross
Dr Giles Davidson
Dr David Gibson
Kate Hare
Graham Hill
Susan Hornby
Dr Angela Hutton
Stephen Hyde
Nick Jones
Sue Jordan
Gill King
Louise Kirby
John Lawson
Linda Martin
Andy Mawe
Andrew McLeod
Joanne Norman
Richard Oades
Gill Pike
Diane Porter
Neil Porteus
Katy Rigby
Emma Roydhouse
Yolanda Ruiz Martinez

Leah-Anne Shillito
Kirsten Stow
Sue Waterhouse

Lead design team
Terry Farrell & Partners

Terry Farrell
Simon Baker
Peter Barbalov
Chris Barber
Mike Barry
Nigel Bidwell
Toby Bridge
John Campbell
Darren Cartlidge
Amy Dunn
Simon Evans
Marta Garriz
Tom Gent
Jo Greenoak
Matt Holder
Moz Hussain
Karl James
Erica Jong
Tom Kimbell
Steve Middleton
Lorraine Mulraney
James Patterson

Aidan Potter
Liz Reilly
Michela Ruffatti
Stefania Salvetti
Roger Simmons
Cherry Sherlock-Tanner
Jason Speechly-Dick
Mike Stowell
Doug Streeter

Helen Thomas
Catriona Thompson
Jane Tobin
Julian Tollast
Hope Wallace

Picture credits

All images courtesy of Terry
Farrell & Partners unless
specified below:

front cover Richard Bryant
www.arcaid.co.uk
inside front cover Hull Daily Mail;
2–3 Richard Bryant
10 Hull Daily Publications Ltd.
11 top and middle: Hull
Maritime Museum
12 Tom Kimbell
14 The Core
15 bottom right: Andrew Putler
20–21 Richard Bryant
23 bottom left: Hamburger
Kunsthalle; photographer: Elke
Walford, Hamburg
23 bottom right: Andrew Putler
30 Andrew Putler
37 Matthew Swift
40–41 John Hewitt
42–43 Richard Bryant
44 Sean Gallagher
45 Sean Gallagher
46 Sean Gallagher
48 Alan Stephen Photography
51 Sean Gallagher

56–57 Richard Bryant
58–59 Richard Bryant
60–61 Richard Bryant
62–63 Richard Bryant
64–65 Richard Bryant
66–67 Richard Bryant
68–69 Richard Bryant
70–71 Richard Bryant
72 Richard Bryant
73 Innes Photographers
74–75 Tim Soar
76–77 Richard Bryant
78–79 Richard Bryant
80 Adam Powell
81 Guzelian
82–83 Guzelian
84 Richard Bryant
85 Tim Soar
86 left Tim Soar
86 right Guzelian
87 Guzelian
88 David Lazenby
89 top and bottom Tim Soar
91 Richard Bryant
92–93 Tim Soar
95 Innes Photographers
inside back cover Tim Soar
back cover Guzelian

Published 2002 by Wordsearch
5 Old Street
London EC1V 9HL
T 020 7549 5400
F 020 7336 8660
ISDN 020 7253 1402
studio@wordsearch.co.uk
www.wordsearch.co.uk

Copyright © Wordsearch
ISBN 0-9532158-3-0

Text:
Hugh Pearman

Book design:
Wordsearch

Photography:
Richard Bryant
Tim Soar
Guzelian

www.thedeep.co.uk
www.terryfarrell.com